Snap books™

Queens and Princesses

GRAND DUCHESS

Anastasia Romanov

by Mary Englar

Consultant:

Thomas Emmert, PhD
Professor of History, Gustavus Adolphus College
St. Peter, Minnesota

Capstone press®

Mankato, Minnesota

Snap Books are published by Capstone Press,
151 Good Counsel Drive, P.O. Box 669, Mankato, Minnesota 56002.
www.capstonepress.com

Library of Congress Cataloging-in-Publication Data
Englar, Mary.
  Grand Duchess Anastasia Romanov / by Mary Englar.
  p. cm. — (Snap books. Queens and princesses).
  Summary: "Describes the life and death of Grand Duchess Anastasia Romanov
of Russia" — Provided by publisher.
  Includes bibliographical references and index.
  ISBN-13: 978-1-4296-1955-4 (hardcover)
  ISBN-10: 1-4296-1955-4 (hardcover)
  1. Anastasia Nikolaevna, Grand Duchess, daughter of Nicholas II, Emperor of
Russia, 1901–1918. 2. Princesses — Russia — Biography. 3. Russia — History —
Nicholas II, 1894–1917. I.Title. II. Series.
DK254.A7E54 2009
947.08'3092 — dc22   2008002909

Editor: Angie Kaelberer
Designer: Juliette Peters
Photo Researcher: Wanda Winch

Photo Credits: Beinecke Rare Book and Manuscript Library, Yale University,
14, 15, 19, 29; Getty Images Inc./AFP/Yuri Kadobnov, 7; Getty Images Inc./Hulton
Archive, 13, 16, 22, 26, 28; Getty Images Inc./Hulton Archive/Topical Press Agency,
25; Getty Images Inc./Popperfoto, cover; Getty Images Inc./Taxi/FPG, 6; Getty
Images Inc./Time & Life Pictures/Mansell, 17; Getty Images Inc./Topical Press
Agency/J. Windhager, 5; The Image Works/HIP/Print Collector, 21; The Image
Works/Roger-Viollet, 10; Mary Evans Picture Library, 9

Essential content terms are **bold** and are defined at the bottom of the page where
they first appear.

1 2 3 4 5 6 13 12 11 10 09 08

Table of Contents

AN *Imperial* FAMILY

On a spring day in May 1913, 11-year-old Grand Duchess Anastasia Romanov stepped from her carriage. She was in the small Russian town of Kostroma. Anastasia joined her three older sisters for the parade to the local church. Dressed in matching white dresses and hats, the four girls lined up behind their parents. Their younger brother rode high in the arms of a tall soldier.

Anastasia's family came from Kostroma. Exactly 300 years before, the first Romanov had been chosen to lead the Russian people. Now Anastasia's parents, **Tsar** Nicholas II and **Tsarina** Alexandra, led the parade. It was one of many events throughout Russia celebrating 300 years of rule by the Romanov family.

Anastasia dressed up for special occasions like dances and parades.

tsar — the Russian emperor
tsarina — the wife of a tsar

5

Anastasia knew what to do on such an important day. From the age of 7, she had attended events with her parents. Anastasia walked slowly. Her back was straight, and she nodded to the thousands of Russians lining the street. Church bells rang out as the crowds cheered.

Anastasia tried to keep her excitement from showing on her face. She held onto her hat as the wind swirled around her. Soldiers marched beside the duchesses to protect them from the crowd.

Anastasia looked at her father, walking straight and proud at the head of the parade. The tsar was the ruler of the Russian Empire, but to Anastasia, he was just Papa.

Anastasia's father, Tsar Nicholas II, ruled the huge Russian Empire.

FABERGÉ EGGS

Peter Carl Fabergé was the official jeweler to Tsar Nicholas and his father. The most famous Fabergé creations were jeweled Easter eggs he designed each year for the tsars. Nicholas gave one to his wife and one to his mother every Easter.

Fabergé had to make each egg new and unique. He put a surprise inside each egg. The eggs opened to reveal a tiny working train, portraits of the tsar's family, or a rooster that crowed and flapped its wings. Of the 56 imperial eggs that Fabergé made, eight have been lost. Only 19 are still in Russia. In 2004, a Russian businessman bought nine of the eggs from a private collection. The eggs were valued between $3 million and $24 million each.

GRAND DUCHESS
Anastasia

Early on the morning of June 18, 1901, Tsarina Alexandra gave birth to her fourth daughter. Anastasia was healthy, with blond hair and blue eyes. Her parents were happy, but they had hoped for a son. In Russia, only a boy could become tsar.

THE RUSSIAN EMPIRE

Anastasia's father ruled one of the largest and wealthiest empires in Europe. The country stretched from eastern Europe to the Pacific Ocean. Tsar Nicholas made all the government decisions. No one in the Russian Empire was allowed to question the tsar or his laws.

The Romanov family was one of richest in the world. They owned millions of acres of land. The family jewels were worth $80 million. When Anastasia's father was crowned in 1896, he sat on a throne decorated with nearly 900 sparkling diamonds.

Tsarina Alexandra gave birth to her fourth daughter, Anastasia, in June 1901.

9

AT HOME IN THE ALEXANDER PALACE

Anastasia's family owned seven palaces. Three palaces were located on 800 acres (324 hectares) of parkland near Russia's capital, St. Petersburg. The land was called the Tsarskoe Selo, or the Tsar's Village. A tall iron fence surrounded the village. Soldiers patrolled the grounds to keep people out.

During the late fall and winter, the family lived at the Alexander Palace in the Tsar's Village. The family seldom used the village's other two palaces, the Catherine Palace and the Bablovo Palace.

The Alexander Palace had more than 100 rooms. Alexandra decorated the family rooms with wallpaper and flowered fabrics. Fresh flowers were everywhere. The children's bedrooms were on the second floor. Their windows looked out on the gardens.

When Anastasia's great-great-grandfather ruled Russia, Alexander Palace's living room was called the Crimson Parlor.

Heavy snow covered the grounds during winter. The children learned to ski, skate, and sled. When the snow melted, they drove pony carts along miles of pathways. A playhouse sat on an island in a lake. The children crossed a bridge to play there.

Anastasia's family loved their quiet life. The four sisters were very close. They had few friends outside of the palace. They knew little about the everyday lives of ordinary Russians.

THE IMPERIAL TRAIN

Anastasia's family traveled around Russia on the royal blue imperial train. Eleven cars made up the train. One car held the bedroom, sitting room, office, and bathroom for Nicholas and Alexandra. The large bathtub had a lip that kept the water from spilling out even when the train was moving. The dining car included a table that sat 20. The kitchen had three stoves and an icebox to keep food cold.

LIFE AS A
Romanov

Anastasia was a tomboy who liked playing games and climbing trees. Her mother nicknamed her "the imp." Anastasia loved to make people laugh. She made faces when her picture was taken and played jokes on her sisters.

Anastasia shared a room with her sister Marie. Marie was two years older than Anastasia. Their parents called them the "Little Pair." Her older sisters, Olga and Tatiana, were the "Big Pair." Olga was six years older than Anastasia, and Tatiana was four years older.

In spite of their family's wealth, Anastasia and her siblings weren't spoiled with luxuries. The children slept on hard cots without pillows. They took cold baths each morning. Then they helped the servants clean the bedrooms and make the beds.

Anastasia (second from right) was very close to her sisters (left to right) Marie, Tatiana, and Olga.

ENDLESS LESSONS

Every morning after breakfast, the children began their lessons. Tutors taught them history, math, geography, Russian, French, and English. Anastasia picked up languages easily. She spoke Russian with her father and English with her mother. The Tsarina had spent much of her childhood in England. But mostly, Anastasia thought lessons were boring.

Nicholas and his children spent an hour outside before lunch, which was their main meal of the day. They all loved to play with the family's 11 collie dogs. In the winter, they built ice hills for sledding.

After lunch, the children continued their lessons. Anastasia's mother also taught the girls music, sewing, and embroidery. Nicholas' sister Olga came often to teach painting. Anastasia loved to paint pictures of flowers and take photos of her family.

Anastasia much preferred playing outside to studying.

Anastasia's mother taught her to knit and embroider at a young age.

FAMILY TIME

Every afternoon at 4:00, the family gathered for tea in Alexandra's mauve sitting room. Anastasia and her sisters wore fresh white dresses with colorful sashes. Tea was served with bread and butter. The children played as their father read newspapers and talked with their mother. As the girls got older, they practiced their embroidery at tea time.

At 8:00 in the evening, the family ate a light supper. This meal was served in the cozy sitting room or the library. The young children went to bed after supper. As they got older, they stayed up until after evening tea at 11:00.

After supper, Nicholas often read aloud books by Russian, French, or English authors. Sometimes the family worked together to glue photographs into family albums. Anastasia decorated her albums with paintings.

A NEW BROTHER

When Anastasia was 3, her mother gave birth to a son, Alexei. Finally the family had a son who would someday rule Russia. Anastasia loved her baby brother's blond curls and blue eyes.

Shortly after Alexei was born, bruises began to appear on his body. The bruises grew into large, purple lumps beneath his skin. His parents learned that he had **hemophilia**. This condition prevents blood from clotting easily. People with hemophilia can bleed to death from cuts, and even minor bruises bleed under the skin. Alexei suffered extreme pain, and there was no cure.

The family welcomed baby Alexei in 1904.

hemophilia — a health condition in which the blood does not clot normally

RASPUTIN

Alexei's doctors had no treatments for his illness. The pain in his joints was terrible, and his parents didn't know what to do. A friend of Alexandra's told her to call on a mysterious holy man who lived in St. Petersburg. Grigori Efimovich Rasputin was a poor peasant from Siberia.

When Rasputin prayed with Alexei, Alexandra noticed that her son suffered less pain. When Alexei's health improved, she believed that Rasputin had healed him through prayer.

Both Nicholas and Alexandra called Rasputin a friend. But many in the royal family did not believe his powers were real. They believed Rasputin had too much influence on the royal family. In 1916, a group of Russian nobles killed Rasputin.

> "Our rooms here (Livadia) are very large and clean and white, and we have real fruit and grapes growing here. I am so happy that we don't have those horrid lessons."
>
> Letter from Anastasia, age 10, to her Russian teacher

FAMILY VACATIONS

Every year in March, Anastasia's family boarded the imperial train for Livadia Palace near the Black Sea. Livadia's white stone walls shone in the warm sun. It was Anastasia's favorite palace. She swam, played tennis, and painted with Aunt Olga. She rode horses and hiked with her father.

Each June, Anastasia's family explored the coast of Finland on their **yacht**, the *Standardt*. The large ship had room for the imperial family, guests, and the royal guards.

Below deck, the sitting rooms and dining rooms had polished wood floors, crystal light fixtures, and velvet drapes. Anastasia and her sisters roamed the sunny deck. They flirted with the handsome young officers. On special occasions, the yacht's band played for the family. Then the girls got the chance to dance with their favorite officers.

yacht — a large boat or small ship used for sailing or racing

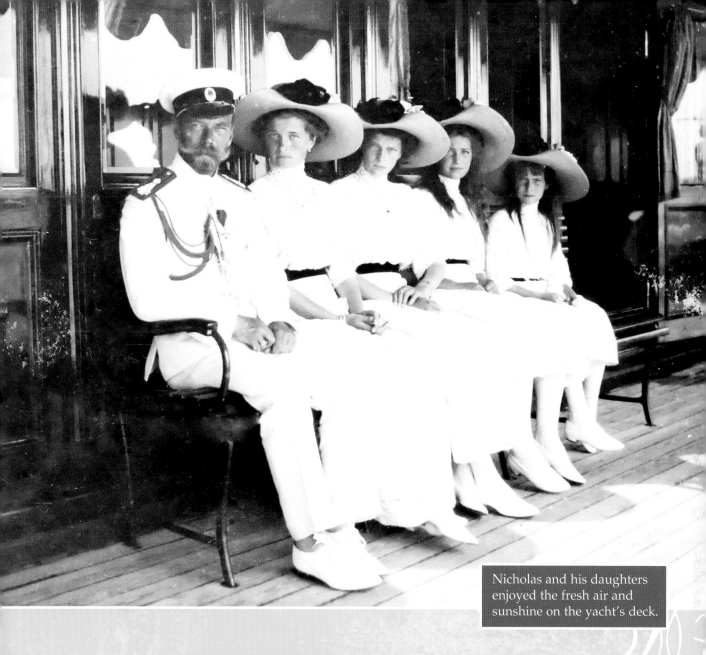

Nicholas and his daughters enjoyed the fresh air and sunshine on the yacht's deck.

Girls in the Romanov family officially entered society when they were 16. Their parents hosted a formal dance called a ball for them. At the ball, Nicholas gave the 16-year-old daughter a diamond and pearl necklace. Alexandra collected jewels every year to make into the necklaces. But Anastasia never got the chance to attend a ball in her honor. A war was coming, and it would change the lives of Anastasia and her family forever.

THE *World* GOES TO *War*

In June 1914, Serbian rebel Gavrilo Princip killed Archduke Franz Ferdinand. The archduke was the future emperor of Austria-Hungary. Austria-Hungary declared war on Serbia a month later. Nicholas knew he had to support Serbia, which was Russia's ally. By early August, Russia declared war on Austria-Hungary and Germany. France and Great Britain sided with Russia. Soon, most of the world was fighting World War I (1914–1918).

Although Russia had a huge army, it did not have modern guns or artillery. Nicholas took charge of the army. He went to the front lines in 1915, which were hundreds of miles from St. Petersburg. He came home when he could. His family visited him when the fighting wasn't too heavy. Anastasia missed her father and wrote to him often.

Anastasia missed her father (center) when he had to go to the Russian front during World War I.

Anastasia (right) and Marie visited wounded Russian soldiers in the hospital.

LIFE ON THE HOME FRONT

During the war, Anastasia, her mother, and her sisters visited wounded soldiers at nearby hospitals. Alexandra, Olga, and Tatiana took nursing classes. Anastasia and Marie were too young to be nurses, but they sat and talked with the soldiers. One of them gave Anastasia her favorite dog, a King Charles spaniel named Jimmy.

During the next three years, 1.3 million Russian soldiers were killed. Another 4.2 million were injured. At home, many Russians were starving. Most of the farmers were serving in the army, and any available food went to feed the soldiers.

On March 8, 1917, people in St. Petersburg broke into bakeries to steal bread. Huge crowds marched in the streets. The loss of so many men and the lack of food led to demonstrations against the tsar. The people blamed Nicholas for their problems. It was the beginning of a **revolution**.

TSAR NICHOLAS RESIGNS

A temporary government took over in the capital. Russia's many political parties couldn't agree on what form of government the country should have. The temporary government finally agreed that Nicholas must resign. Even Nicholas' generals asked him to step down. They feared a civil war would break out.

On March 15, Nicholas resigned at the army's headquarters in the city of Pskov. He did not want Russia to fall apart. He hoped that his resignation would end the protests.

revolution — an uprising by a group of people against a system of government or a way of life

THE END OF
Russian Royalty

Anastasia, her mother, and her siblings waited anxiously for Nicholas to return to the palace. The trains had stopped running, so they had no idea when he would come. The situation at the palace wasn't good, either. The electricity, water, and telephones were cut off. The palace guards and many of the servants had fled. Anastasia and her sisters were sick with the measles.

Nicholas finally returned to Alexander Palace on March 22. He told his family he had resigned. Anastasia's parents didn't know if the new government would let the family stay in Russia.

In 1916, Anastasia (second from right) enjoyed a day with her family and cousins. A year later, the happy times were over for the Romanovs.

ONE LAST YEAR

Anastasia and her family spent the last year of their lives under house arrest. Soldiers guarded them and wouldn't allow them to leave the palace. In August 1917, the family was moved to a house in Tobolsk, Siberia. The family tried to live a normal life. The children studied, celebrated holidays, and wrote letters to their friends.

In October 1917, the Bolshevik Party overthrew the temporary government. This party wanted to form a communist government where the land and wealth belonged to all the Russian people. The Bolsheviks especially disliked Nicholas. They thought he didn't care about the needs of the Russian people.

In Siberia, Nicholas and his children enjoyed the sun on the roof of a greenhouse.

"For now, good–bye. I wish you the best, happiness, and all good things. We constantly pray for you and think, help us Lord . . . I embrace all of you tightly and kiss you."

Letter from Anastasia to a friend, 1918

In spring 1918, the family was moved to the town of Yekaterinburg in central Russia. At night, the family could hear guns in the distance. The family didn't know it, but the gunfire came from the White Army. These soldiers were trying to rescue the tsar and his family.

SENTENCED TO DEATH

At midnight on July 17, 1918, the commander of the guards woke the family. He ordered them to get dressed. In a small basement room, he told them to line up for a photograph. He said that he needed proof that the tsar had not escaped.

A few minutes later, armed guards filled the small room. The commander told Nicholas that he and his family had been sentenced to death by the Bolshevik government. Then the guards opened fire. Anastasia, her family, their doctor, and their servants were all killed. The guards burned their bodies and buried the remains in a secret place.

A week later, the White Army reached Yekaterinburg. At the house, all they found was Alexei's half-starved spaniel, Joy. The soldiers believed the family had been killed, but they had no proof. It would be many years before the Bolshevik government admitted that they had ordered the Romanovs' deaths.

THE MYSTERY OF ANNA ANDERSON

For many years, no one was sure if Anastasia's family had been killed. One rumor said the family was living in the United States. Other rumors said one of the girls escaped from the basement room. Many women claimed to be Anastasia.

One claim seemed to have some truth in it. In 1920, a young woman tried to kill herself by jumping off a bridge in Berlin, Germany. A police officer rescued her and took her to a hospital. The woman refused to tell her name or anything else about herself. Her doctors gave her the name Anna Anderson. Nearly two years later, Anna Anderson said she really was Anastasia Romanov.

People who knew the real Anastasia disagreed about this strange woman. Some believed her, while others called her a liar. Anderson stuck to her story until she died in 1984. In 1994, scientists compared a DNA sample from Anderson to the Romanov skeletons. It finally proved that Anna Anderson was not Anastasia.

DISCOVERY OF THE SECRET GRAVE

The mystery of what happened to Anastasia and her family took more than 70 years to solve. A grave was discovered in a forest near Yekaterinburg in 1979. In 1991, researchers dug up the bones. They performed DNA tests on the bones in 1994. Scientists were certain that the bones belonged to Nicholas, Alexandra, and three of their daughters. They could not agree if the smallest skeleton was Anastasia or Marie.

The skeletons of Alexei and one of the girls were missing from the grave. In the summer of 2007, a second grave was found near the first. The grave held the bones of two people, but they were badly burned. In 2008, DNA tests proved that the bones were those of Alexei and Marie. Anastasia was buried in the other grave.

Anastasia had just celebrated her 17th birthday when she died. Her love of life made her a favorite of all who met her. Today Anastasia is remembered as a young woman whose life ended much too soon.

Until the end of her life, Anastasia loved being outdoors.

Glossary

Bolshevik (BOWL-shuh-vik) — a member of the political party that took power in Russia in 1917

communist (KAHM-yuh-nist) — having to do with supporting communism; communism is a way of organizing a country so that all the land, houses, and factories belong to the government or community.

duchess (DUHCH-iss) — the title used in Anastasia's family for princess

hemophilia (hee-muh-FIL-ee-uh) — a health condition where blood does not clot normally

imperial (im-PIHR-ee-uhl) — relating to an empire or emperor

resign (ri-ZINE) — to give up a position or a job

revolution (rev-uh-LOO-shun) — an uprising by a group of people against a system of government or a way of life

tsar (ZAHR) — the Russian emperor

tsarina (zah-REE-nuh) — the wife of a tsar

yacht (YOT) — a large boat or small ship used for sailing or racing

Read More

Bjornlund, Britta. *The Russian Revolution.* People at the Center of. Detroit: Blackbirch Press, 2005.

Hintz, Martin. *Russia.* True Book. New York: Children's Press, 2004.

Meyer, Carolyn. *Anastasia, The Last Grand Duchess.* Royal Diaries. New York: Scholastic, 2000.

Internet Sites

FactHound offers a safe, fun way to find Internet sites related to this book. All of the sites on FactHound have been researched by our staff.

Here's how:

1. Visit *www.facthound.com*
2. Choose your grade level.
3. Type in this book ID **1429619554** for age-appropriate sites. You may also browse subjects by clicking on letters, or by clicking on pictures and words.
4. Click on the **Fetch It** button.

FactHound will fetch the best sites for you!

Index